MW01194542

kim

love is...

...in bloom

Kim Casali

Abrams Image
New York

love is...

love is...

Introduction

Love Is. . . still in bloom! Now over thirty-five years since it first appeared in the *Los Angeles Times*, the cartoon remains a beloved fixture in popular culture. Its simple truths and universal themes have reached millions the world over and remain as fresh and original today as they were so many years ago.

Begun in the 1960s in the heart of a shy artist, the first cartoons were actually Kim Grove's private little "love notes" to her future husband, Roberto Casali.

She would leave her tender sentiments for him everywhere—in the pocket of his jeans, under his pillow, on the seat of his car, even in his sock drawer. Unbeknownst to her, Roberto kept each and every one of them. Believing his wife's drawings to be something exceptional, he decided to show them to a contact in the syndication business who agreed that they should be made public. And so the Love Is. . . phenomenon was born.

But how is love born? As for Kim and Roberto, it starts with a glance, a smile, or an inkling that a certain someone is in fact "that special someone." Over time, through life's ups and downs, it becomes as much about the little things as the big ones—from the day-to-day to the life transforming. Indeed, it sometimes requires compromise. But no matter what, when two hearts are afire, Love Is. . . and will always be. . . the spice of life.

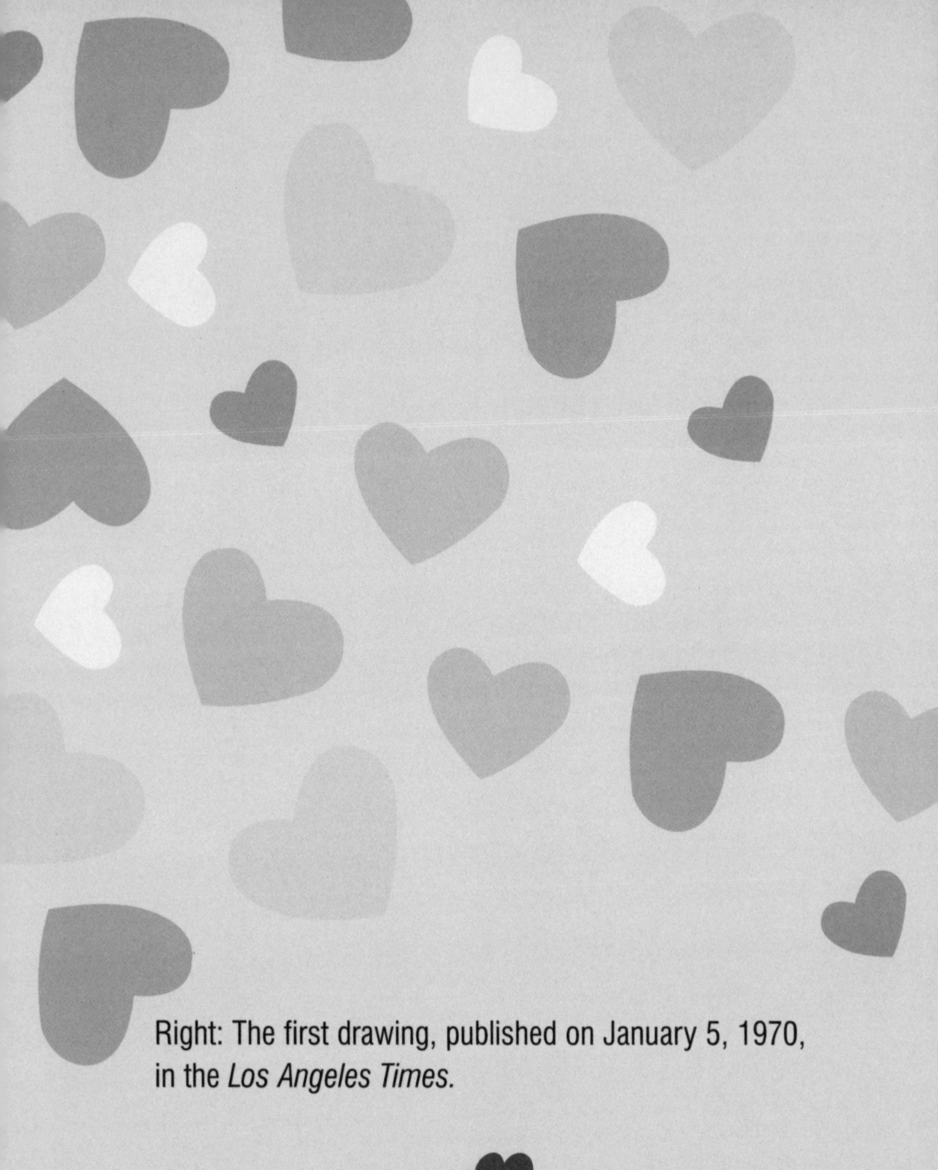

Right: The first drawing, published on January 5, 1970, in the *Los Angeles Times.*

love is...

...not picking the most expensive dish on the menu

love is...

...finding that someone special

love is...

...noticing you've been noticed

love is...

...making her a queen

love is...

...a long weekend—and you!

love is...

...the best thing that ever happened to you

love is...

...someone to watch over you

love is...

Kim

...being in tune

love is...

...when the whole world seems right

love is...

...making you feel young again

love is...

...having someone to sit with by the fire

love is...

...better than fame
and fortune

love is...

...when his world revolves around you

love is...

...being all wrapped up in each other

love is...

...intuition

love is...

...a touch of first-night nerves

love is...

...a tender look

love is...

...having designs on her

love is...

...feeling secure in dangerous waters

love is...

...knowing you have the right partner

love is...

...someone you can’t forget

love is...

...the way only he can kiss

love is...

...when you can't bear to let him go

love is...

...something you can't keep a secret any longer

love is...

...feeling self-conscious when you meet

love is...

...when nothing can dampen your spirits

love is...

...clicking

love is...

...being in the right place at the right time

love is...

...making the first move

love is...

...looking your future in the face

love is...

...finding your soul mate

love is...

...a rare find

love is...

...someone who floats into your life

love is...

...your sixth sense

love is...

...wondering if this could be it

love is...

...someone who makes you weak in the knees

love is...

...something right out of your wildest dreams

love is...

...a great attraction

love is...

...getting the right signal

love is...

...when the writing is on the wall

love is...

...a rare and precious thing

love is...

...choosing you from everyone

love is...

...when she's your pearl

love is...

...being his "first lady"

love is...

...that feeling of "butterflies" when you meet

love is...

...meeting your match

...what causes you to lose your concentration

love is...

...thanking her for coming into your life

love is...

...when you can't get him out of your head

love is...

...when your future is crystal clear

love is...

...a fan club of two

love is...

...ignoring all the other boys

love is...

...like winning the jackpot

love is...

...when something special happens

love is...

...when lightning strikes twice

love is...

...being the right person for someone

love is...

...giving her the look that says it all

love is...

...a step in the right direction

love is...

...that certain smile

love is...

...pinching yourself to make sure it's real

love is...

...bound to happen sooner or later

love is...

...a feeling that grows and blossoms

love is...

...seeing her face everywhere

love is...

...seeing him in your future

love is...

...the story of two people

love is...

...seeing each other in
a new light

love is...

...someone you'd follow to the ends of the earth

love is...

...making sure she's not the one who got away

love is...

...sharing experiences together

love is...

...having someone to hug

love is...

...a blossoming romance

love is...

...growing together

love is...

...choosing the right
road together

love is...

...wondering what the future holds

love is...

...enjoying the high life together

love is...

...understanding each other

love is...

...a glimpse of what might be

love is...

...a first birthday

love is...

...making marriage work

love is...

...communicating

love is...

...thinking of the future

love is...

...seeing in the new year together

love is...

...helping her through life's
"ups" and "downs"

love is...

...caring when the going gets hard

love is...

...making a house a home

love is...

...telling her she's the pick of the bunch

love is...

...the journey of a lifetime

love is...

...making an effort to understand her

love is...

...your vision of tomorrow

love is...

...my promise to you

love is...

...standing the test of time

love is...

...reaping the love that you've sown

love is...

...a feeling that grows with the years

love is...

...a little wonder

love is...

...when spring is just around the corner

love is...

...a chain reaction

love is...

...doing things together

love is...

...coming home safely

love is...
...seeing him as a father

love is...

...sitting together and
saying nothing

love is...

...being a proud father

love is...

...something you have to look after

love is...

...when three is company

love is...

...when he becomes more attentive

love is...

...paving the way to happiness

love is...

...helping to make the world a better place

love is...

...a great adventure

love is...

...building her dream castle

love is...

...what links your future

love is...

...counting the days
you're apart

love is...

...learning the ropes

love is...

...bringing out the best in each other

love is...

...making it work with more positives than negatives

love is...

...showing her the house where you spent your childhood

love is...

...being open with each other

love is...

...sitting up all night with a sick child

love is...

...needing you

love is...

...when the days draw in, and you draw closer

love is...

...looking forward to long winter nights together

love is...

...when the passion slows down and the friendship speeds up

love is...

...more than just skin deep

love is...

...feeling richer than millionaires

love is...

...seeing his face beside yours every morning

love is...

...attention to the little things

love is...

...fussing over each other

love is...

...buying her a soft toy

love is...

...the right word

love is...

...telling her she looks wonderful on a down day

love is...

Kim

...letting her cut your prize roses

love is...

...a sigh

love is...

...indulging his tall stories

love is...

...listening to his snoring and pretending it's music

love is...

...the warmth of his smile

love is...

...hot chicken soup when you're feeling low

love is...

...a smile

love is...

...saying you like her new hat

love is...

...always thinking of her

love is...

...phoning to see if she's all right

love is...

...remembering to tape her favorite program

love is...

...someone who never forgets your birthday

love is...

...letting her warm her feet on yours

love is...

Kim

...doing little things for each other

love is...

...taking your boots off before coming in

love is...

...someone who phones to say goodnight

love is...

...a rickshaw ride together

love is...

...letting her have the first bite

love is...

...scratching an itch she can't reach

love is...

...knowing exactly what he wants

love is...

...a daily hug

love is...

...knowing he remembered

love is...

...taking turns cooking

love is...

...not leaving the newspaper
a mess

love is...

...knowing her number by heart

love is...

...giving her flowers again

love is...

...running her bath for her

love is...

...a big smile

love is...

...a bedtime story

love is...

...washing up without being asked

love is...

...being her handyman

love is...

...shopping sensibly when he's on a diet

love is...

...thinking of someone other than yourself

love is...

...kissing the hurt away

love is...

...having someone to cuddle

love is...

...hearing him say he loves you

love is...

...giving him "one for the road"

love is...

...knowing his innermost thoughts

love is...

...always caring

love is...

...looking the best for the man in your life

love is...

...the way he smiles at you

love is...

...the thought that counts

love is...

...making tea for two

love is...

...showing you care

love is...

...holding her hand during takeoff

love is...

...having a man at your feet

love is...

...seeing her home safely

love is...

...a goodnight kiss from Mummy

love is...

...hiding a love note in his fishing box

love is...

...massaging those tension knots

love is...

...remembering by listening to "golden oldies"

love is...

...going fishing, together

love is...

...helping her unwind

love is...

...taking her out for Sunday brunch

love is...

...counting every single freckle

love is...

...helping around the house without having to be asked

love is...

...someone to brush your hair

love is...

...taking them on a roller coaster ride

love is...

...doing the ironing

love is...

...keeping a light burning for him

love is...

...keeping a picture of her at work

love is...

...staying up late to wrap his presents

love is...

...knitting him a sweater

love is...

...giving each other silly pet names

love is...

...when everything's for two

love is...

...someone to keep you warm

love is...

...making him feel good about himself

love is...

...a subscription to his favorite car magazine

love is...

...enjoying a close encounter in the rain

love is...

...sometimes having to compromise

love is...

...giving her more of the umbrella on a rainy day

love is...

GRRR!

...not taking your anger out on him

love is...

...never criticizing his ex-wife

love is...

...not being isolated by your phone, fax, and computer

love is...

...not stepping on his emotions

love is...

...not wearing overpowering aftershave

love is...

...a waiting game

love is...

...taking care of the repairs with a smile

love is...

...asking him nicely—not giving orders

love is...

kim

...taking off your headphones
when she's talking

love is...

...narrowing it down to one

love is...

...not hiding things from each other

love is...

...when he doesn't flinch at the price

love is...

...overcoming all obstacles

love is...

...sometimes having to control your urge to shop

love is...

...not complaining when his sports car ruins your hairdo

love is...

...something you have to work at

love is...

...taking it—lying down

love is...

...not always pointing an accusing finger

love is...

YAK!
YAK!
YAK!

...being a good listener

love is...

...not raking up the past like dead leaves

love is...

...letting him wear his favorite old jacket

love is...

...being willing to compromise

love is...

...taking turns when the baby needs feeding

love is...

...doing the shopping together

love is...

...making up

love is...

...putting it your way but nicely

love is...

...not taking your cell phone to dinner

love is...

...sometimes a balancing act

love is...

...trying not to show your anger

love is...

...trying to be patient

love is...

...coming down from your ivory tower

love is...

...knowing when he needs a little space

love is...

...sharing the driving

love is...

...not asking how much her new dress cost

love is...

...letting him drive with the top down

love is...

...helping her rearrange the furniture—again!

love is...

...not always talking business when you're together

love is...

...trying to understand her kind of music

love is...

...having it out, then forgetting it

love is...

...doing the shopping when you'd rather be fishing

love is...

...not being a backseat driver

love is...

...making sacrifices

love is...

...never letting the sun set on your anger

love is...

...not making fun of his taste

love is...

...waiting for her—even in bad weather

love is...

...trying to see the other point of view

love is...

...trying to forget his faults

love is...

...letting her get it off her chest

love is...

...patching up a quarrel

love is...

...doing things for her

love is...

...two hearts afire

love is...

...blowing her a kiss

love is...

...throwing caution to the wind

love is...

...being in the dark together

love is...

...what blows the cobwebs away

...using your imagination

love is...

...being together again

love is...

...supper by candlelight

love is...

...sometimes running aground

love is...

...a touch of spring fever

love is...

...all yours!

love is...

...when you can't tear yourself away

love is...

...getting up late on
Saturday morning

love is...

...like dynamite—very explosive

love is...

WUTHERING HEIGHTS

...curling up with a good book—together

love is...
...getting him all steamed up

love is...

...getting passionate

love is...

...whisking her off to romantic places

love is...

...changing from jeans to a dress

love is...

...when he loses his reserve

love is...

...a dozen red roses

love is...

...being romantics

love is...

...a touch of romance

love is...

...when anything can happen

love is...

...showering her with kisses

love is...

...clearing a path to her door

love is...

...saying a long "good-bye"

love is...

...heart shaped

love is...

...champagne at six

love is...

...being permanently engaged

love is...

...starting off with a kiss

love is...
Kim
...being pampered

love is...

...keeping warm together

love is...

...giving him a “double”

love is...

...wanting to be alone with him

love is...

...living alone with you on a desert island

love is...

...lunch, dinner, and breakfast, together

...tall, dark, and good-looking

love is...

...disturbing his routine

love is...

...a powerful force

love is...

...massaging her toes

love is...

...fluttering your eyelashes at him

love is...

...very effective!

love is...

...thinking of him every night

love is...

...when one kiss is never enough

love is...
...showing her your
romantic moves
Kim

love is...

...someone squeezing your hand

love is...

...calling each other names

love is...

...leaving you breathless

love is...

...mooning over each other

love is...

...a flirty look

love is...

...scenting she's near

love is...

...a blending of romance and friendship

love is...

...sometimes too hot to handle

love is...

...days of wine and roses

love is...

...telepathic!

love is...

...getting all steamed up

love is...

...presents of silk and satin

love is...

...wishing the evening would go on forever

love is...

...doing a little moonlighting

love is...

...the spice of life

love is...

...when you keep hearing bells

love is...

...the "zing" in your life

love is...
Kim
...the way he looks at you

love is...

...letting him hear your heartbeat over the phone

love is...

...within your reach

love is...

...more precious than jewels

love is...

...what makes a happy home

love is...

...the key

love is...

...home, where your heart is!

love is...

...a merry-go-round

love is...

...a time to remember

love is...

...feeling you could touch the stars

love is...

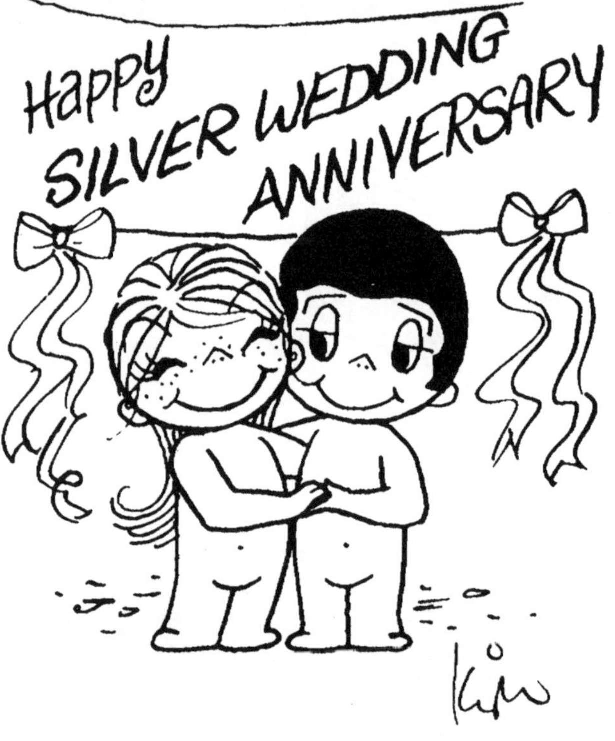

HAPPY
SILVER WEDDING
ANNIVERSARY

...a milestone

love is...

...like wine, better as it matures

love is...

...the sound of her voice

love is...

kim

...the oldest story

love is...

...the sweetest thing

love is...

...taking a chance

love is...

...playing it with passion

love is...

...the twinkle in his eye

love is...

...big news!

love is...

...a symphony for two players

love is...

...an affair of the heart

love is...

...your passport to happiness

love is...

...a store of happy memories

love is...

...what surrounds you

love is...

Kim

...like music to your ears

love is...

...something you would never swap

love is...

...the reason we're together

love is...

kim

...radiating an inner warmth

love is...

...the best thing in your life

love is...

...the warmth in a relationship

Kim

love is...
...heaven sent

love is...

Kim

...your choice

love is...

...when you’re near me

love is...

...always being there

love is...

...a little bit of heaven

love is...

...the end of the line

love is...

...what shapes our lives

love is...

...a new horizon

love is...

...two hearts united

love is...

...when the only view you notice is 'him'

love is...

...hanging out together

love is...

...everywhere

Design by Celina Carvalho
Production Manager: Kaija Markoe

Library of Congress Cataloging-in-Publication Data:

Casali, Kim, 1941-1997.
Love Is... in bloom / Kim Casali.
p. cm.
ISBN-13: 978-0-8109-4922-5
ISBN-10: 0-8109-4922-9
1. Love—Caricatures and cartoons. 2. American wit and humor, Pictorial.
I. Title.

NC1429.G78A4 2006
741.5'3543—dc22
2006013572

Published in 2007 by Abrams Image, an imprint of Harry N. Abrams, Inc.

Printed and bound in China
10 9 8 7 6 5 4 3 2 1

harry n. abrams, inc.
a subsidiary of La Martinière Groupe

115 West 18th Street
New York, NY 10011
www.hnabooks.com